# Graphs, Charts & Tables
## That Build Real-Life Math Skills

by Denise Kiernan

SCHOLASTIC
**PROFESSIONAL BOOKS**

New York • Toronto • London • Auckland • Sydney
Mexico City • New Delhi • Hong Kong • Buenos Aires

Some of the activities in this book were inspired by Scholastic *Math* and *DynaMath*. If you would like to order class subscriptions to these magazines, please call 1-800-724-6527.

Cover design by Jim Sarfati
Cover illustrations by Dave Clegg
Interior design by Melinda Belter
Interior illustrations by Teresa Anderko

ISBN 0-439-11107-2

# Table of Contents

# Introduction

**Statistics are everywhere,** from box scores and stock reports in the newspaper, to food labels in the supermarket, and locations on maps. And everywhere you find them, there's a practical way to teach your students with examples from the real world.

The activities in this book, written with the NCTM (National Council of Teachers of Mathematics) Principles and Standards 2000 in mind, cover a wide variety of visual representations of statistical information in easy-to-use reproducible format. Extension activities give each lesson even more use. Many extension activities can be done over and over, and often take the lessons beyond the classroom.

Each activity features a page for the teacher that explains the activity in detail and gives teaching suggestions. The accompanying reproducible page for the student can be used for test review, given as homework, or assigned as extra credit.

The extension activities also provide learning beyond the classroom. Many of the exercises in this book are taken from everyday life, giving the students many opportunities to apply what they've learned and find related lessons even when they're not at school. The extension activities can be used as longer-term individual or group projects. However you choose to use the activities, students are provided with example after example of the important part that math plays in the world around them.

We hope these activities motivate and inspire your students to become more aware of the world of math in which they live, and give you additional options as you guide them throughout the school year.

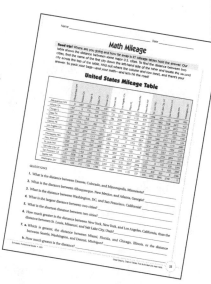

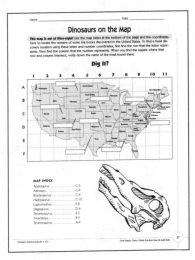

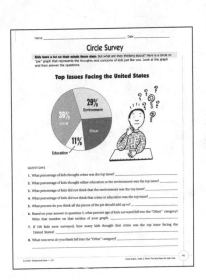

# Math Naps

## Learning Objective
### Students learn to use bar graphs

### DIRECTIONS

1. Distribute the Math Naps reproducible to students and explain that they will be reading a bar graph and comparing the amounts of time different animals spend sleeping.

2. Review bar graphs with students. Explain that these graphs often are used to show and compare total numbers of things; in this case, the total numbers of hours slept.

3. Instruct students to look at the information already graphed for them. They should notice bars are often placed on the graph in ascending or descending order. They should keep this in mind as they complete the graph.

4. Explain to students that after reading the information in the stats box, they should decide where to place each bar and choose a different color to represent each animal they graph.

### ANSWERS

Completed graph should look like this:

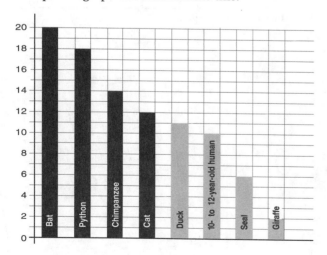

**1a.** 18  **1b.** 12  **1c.** 14  **2.** 10  **3.** Bat, Python, Chimpanzee
**4.** Cat  **5.** Chimpanzee

## What You'll Need

- Math Naps reproducible, page 7

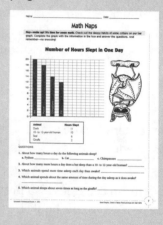

- pencil

- different colored pens or pencils

## EXTENSION ACTIVITY

An adult human sleeps an average of 8 hours a day, while a human baby sleeps 16 hours per day. Ask students to create a bar graph showing this, along with the number of hours per day that they sleep. Ask students if they sleep more or less than the average 10- to 12-year-old.

# Math Naps

**Hey—wake up! It's time for some math.** Check out the sleepy habits of some critters on our bar graph. Complete the graph with the information in the box and answer the questions. And remember—no snoozing!

## Number of Hours Slept in One Day

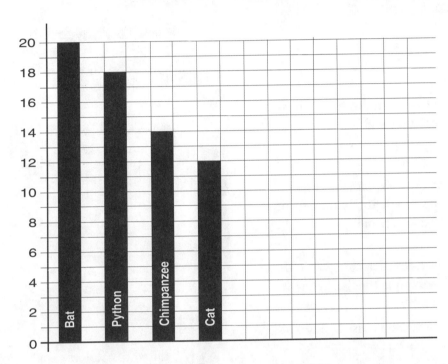

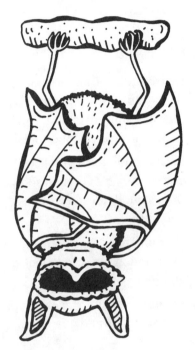

| Animal | Hours Slept |
| --- | --- |
| Duck | 11 |
| 10- to 12-year-old human | 10 |
| Seal | 6 |
| Giraffe | 2 |

QUESTIONS

1. About how many hours a day do the following animals sleep?

   **a.** Python _____  **b.** Cat _____  **c.** Chimpanzee _____

2. About how many more hours a day does a bat sleep than a 10- to 12-year-old human? _____

3. Which animals spend more time asleep each day than awake? _____

4. Which animal spends about the same amount of time during the day asleep as it does awake?

   _____

5. Which animal sleeps about seven times as long as the giraffe? _____

Scholastic Professional Books • 2001

Great Graphs, Charts & Tables That Build Real-Life Math Skills

# Graphs Good Enough to Eat

## Learning Objective

Students learn to use double bar graphs

### DIRECTIONS

1. Distribute the Graphs Good Enough to Eat reproducible to students and explain that in this activity they will be creating double bar graphs to chart information based on survey results about the favorite foods of kids their age.

2. Review double bar graphs with students. Explain that these graphs are often used to show and compare total numbers of things but that each group is divided into two; in this case, boys and girls.

3. Encourage students to read the results of each category in the information box and to look at the example that is already graphed.

4. For each remaining category, students should use a different color for boys and girls to complete the graph.

### ANSWERS

Completed graph should look like this:

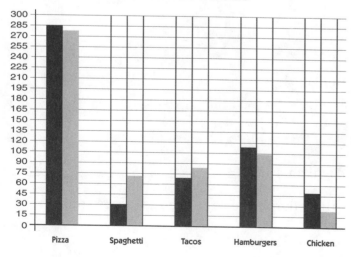

**Fave Lunch Foods**

1. 222   2. Pizza   3. Spaghetti   4. Chicken   5. 14

▲▲▲▲▲▲▲▲

## What You'll Need

- Graphs Good Enough to Eat reproducible, page 9

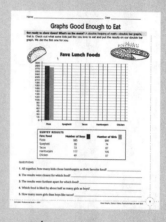

- pencil

- two different colored pens or pencils

▼▼▼▼▼▼▼▼

## EXTENSION ACTIVITY

Take a survey in the classroom or in the school cafeteria about favorite foods and create a double bar graph based on the results. The same kind of survey and resulting graph can be made based on favorite sports, historical figures, colors, television shows—you name it. And the double bar graph does not have to be divided according to gender: It can, for example, compare two classrooms or two different grades.

# Graphs Good Enough to Eat

**Get ready to chow down! What's on the menu?** A double helping of math—double bar graphs, that is. Check out what some kids just like you love to eat and put the results on our double bar graph. We did the first one for you.

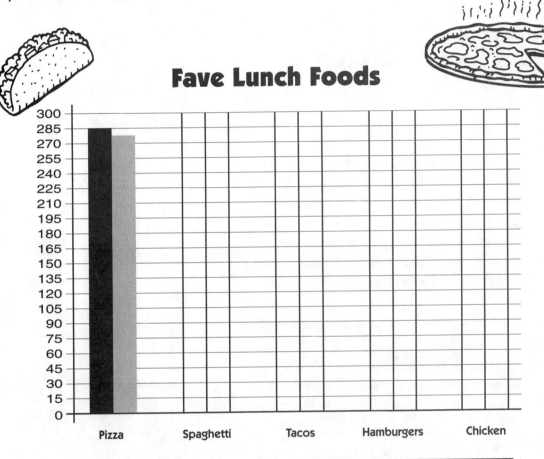

**Fave Lunch Foods**

| SURVEY RESULTS | | |
|---|---|---|
| **Fave Food** | **Number of Boys** ■ | **Number of Girls** ▨ |
| Pizza | 285 | 280 |
| Spaghetti | 32 | 74 |
| Tacos | 73 | 87 |
| Hamburgers | 117 | 105 |
| Chicken | 49 | 27 |

QUESTIONS

1. All together, how many kids chose hamburgers as their favorite food? _____

2. The results were closest for which food? _____

3. The results were furthest apart for which food? _____

4. Which food is liked by about half as many girls as boys? _____

5. How many more girls than boys like tacos? _____

# Pie Time

## Learning Objective

Students learn to use circle or "pie" graphs

### DIRECTIONS

1. Distribute the Pie Time reproducible to students. Explain that they will be reading and creating circle graphs to illustrate how they, other kids their age, and their classmates spend time.

2. Review circle graphs with students and explain that they are used to show parts of a whole. Like a pie cut into pieces, students can look at the size of each piece to understand statistical information. The pie represents all kids surveyed, each piece represents the number of kids.

3. Instruct students to look at the pie and talk about the results before answering the questions.

4. Students will then create a pie graph using the information in the box at the bottom of the page. If possible, students should use a different color to represent each piece of their pie graph.

### ANSWERS

1. 56   2. 88   3. 12

4. The number of kids who play for less than one hour

5. Completed graph should look like this:

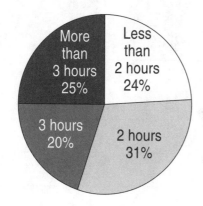

## What You'll Need

- Pie Time reproducible, page 11

- pencil

- different colored pens or pencils

## EXTENSION ACTIVITY

Students can create a circle graph where the whole represents one day and each piece represents the amount of time they spend doing various activities, including sleeping, eating with their families, and so forth. It is an excellent way, while driving home important math concepts, to get students to think about how they spend their time. Two different graphs can be done, one representing a typical school day and one representing a typical summer vacation day.

# Pie Time

**Whole-y circle graphs! Video games are big time**—but how much time do some kids your age spend playing them every day? Look at this circle graph to find out. How big would be your piece of this mathematical pie? Start by answering questions and then bake—er . . . make—a pie of your own using the information at the bottom of the page.

## How Much Time Kids Spend Playing Video Games Each Day
**(Numbers Out of 100 Kids)**

1 hour
29 kids

Less than
1 hour
44 kids

2 hours
15 kids

3 hours
6 kids

4 to 5 hours
4 kids

6 or more hours
2 kids

QUESTIONS

1. How many kids spend at least one hour playing video games?

   _____

2. How many kids spend no more than two hours playing video games?

   _____

3. How many kids spend three or more hours playing video games?

   _____

4. Which is greater: the number of kids who spend two or more hours per day playing video games, or the number of kids who play for less than one hour?

   _____

   _____

5. Now create and label your own circle graph using the following information:

### TIME KIDS SPEND PLAYING SPORTS EACH DAY

| Number of Hours | Percentage of Kids |
| --- | --- |
| Less than 2 | 24 |
| 2 | 31 |
| 3 | 20 |
| More than 3 | 25 |

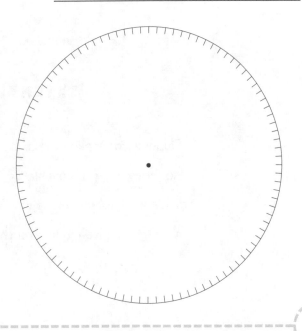

# Stacking Up Stats

## Learning Objective
Students learn to use stacked bar graphs

### What You'll Need

- Stacking Up Stats reproducible, page 13

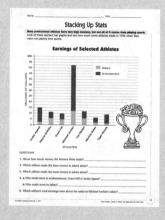

- pencil

- two different colored pens or pencils

## DIRECTIONS

1. Distribute the Stacking Up Stats reproducible to students. Explain that they will be using stacked bar graphs to compare the amount of money athletes make from their salary to the amount they make from endorsements such as television commercials.

2. Review stacked bar graphs with students and explain that they are used to divide one piece of information into two or more parts. In this case, a stacked bar graph divides the total amount of money an athlete makes into salary and endorsements.

3. Instruct students to look at the graph and talk about what they see before answering the questions.

## ANSWERS

1. $7 million
2. Tiger Woods
3. Michael Jordan

4a. Andre Agassi
4b. Grant Hill
5. Cal Ripken

## EXTENSION ACTIVITY

Students can make stacked bar graphs to describe a variety of things that have two components. For example: Those who have savings can divide the total into money they have earned and money that has been given to them such as an allowance or a gift.

# Stacking Up Stats

**Many professional athletes have very high incomes, but not all of it comes from playing sports.** Look at these stacked bar graphs and see how much some athletes made in 1996 when they were not playing their sports.

## Earnings of Selected Athletes

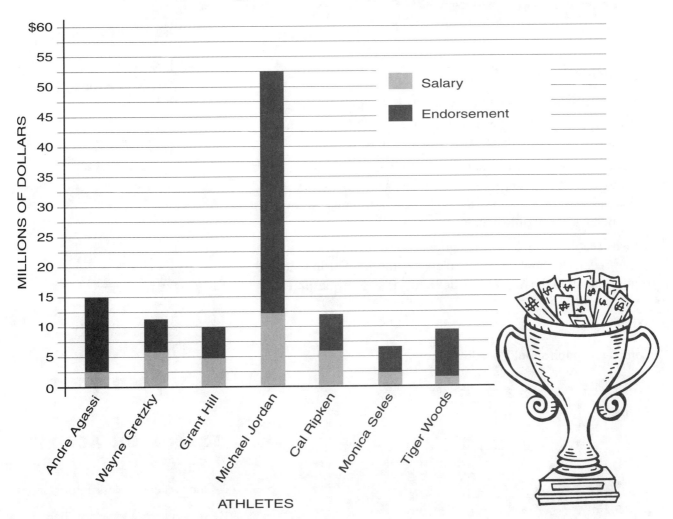

QUESTIONS

1. About how much money did Monica Seles make? _____

2. Which athlete made the least money in salary alone? _____

3. Which athlete made the most money in salary alone? _____

4. **a.** Who made more in endorsements, Grant Hill or Andre Agassi? _____

    **b.** Who made more in salary? _____

5. Which athlete's total earnings were about the same as Michael Jordan's salary? _____

Scholastic Professional Books • 2001          Great Graphs, Charts & Tables That Build Real-Life Math Skills

# Math Movie Madness (Part 1)

## Learning Objective

Students learn to use line graphs

### DIRECTIONS

1. Distribute the Math Movie Madness (Part 1) reproducible to students. Explain that they will be using line graphs to look at how attendance at movie theaters has changed over the years.

2. Review line graphs with students and explain that line graphs are used to show changes over time for a particular statistic. In this case, the line graph will show changes over time for movie attendance in the United States.

3. Instruct students to look at the graph and comment on what they see. They should then complete the line graph using the information in the Attendance box and answer the questions.

### ANSWERS

Completed graph should look like this:

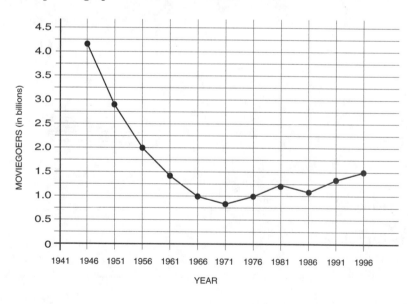

1. 2 billion    2. 1971    3. about 1 billion

4a. 1946 and 1951    4b. 1.3 billion

## What You'll Need

- Math Movie Madness (Part 1) reproducible, page 15

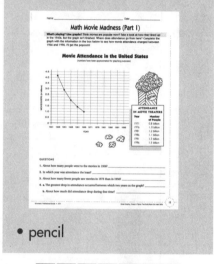

- pencil

## EXTENSION ACTIVITY

Students can gather information from a local theater or theaters about how their attendance has changed over the years. As a discussion topic or essay subject, have students write about how they think video rentals and cable movie channels have affected attendance at movie theaters.

# Math Movie Madness (Part 1)

**What's playing? Line graphs!** Think movies are popular now? Take a look at how they lined up in the 1940s. But the graph isn't finished. Where does attendance go from here? Complete the graph with the information in the box below to see how movie attendance changed between 1966 and 1996. I'll get the popcorn!

## Movie Attendance in the United States

(numbers have been approximated for graphing purposes)

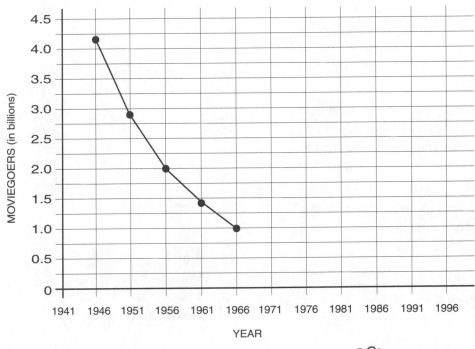

| ATTENDANCE IN MOVIE THEATERS | |
|---|---|
| **Year** | **Number of People** |
| 1971 | 0.8 billion |
| 1976 | 1.0 billion |
| 1981 | 1.2 billion |
| 1986 | 1.1 billion |
| 1991 | 1.3 billion |
| 1996 | 1.5 billion |

QUESTIONS

1. About how many people went to the movies in 1956? _____

2. In which year was attendance the least? _____

3. About how many fewer people saw movies in 1976 than in 1956? _____

4. **a.** The greatest drop in attendance occurred between which two years on the graph? _____

   **b.** About how much did attendance drop during that time? _____

# Math Movie Madness (Part 2)

## Learning Objective

Students learn to use line graphs

### DIRECTIONS

1. Distribute the Math Movie Madness (Part 2) reproducible to students. Explain that they will again use a line graph to look at the world of movies, this time to show how the cost of attending a movie has changed over the years.

2. Review line graphs and the previous activity with students and remind them that line graphs show changes over time for a particular statistic. In this case, the line graph will show changes over time for the cost of movie attendance in the United States.

3. Instruct students to look at the graph and comment on what they see. They should then complete the line graph with the information in the Now Playing box and answer the questions.

### ANSWERS

Completed graph should look like this:

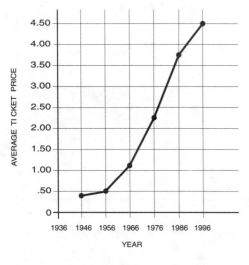

1. $3.25  2. 1976–1986  3. $4.00
4. 1 ticket in 1996  5. 9

## What You'll Need

- Math Movie Madness (Part 2) reproducible, page 17

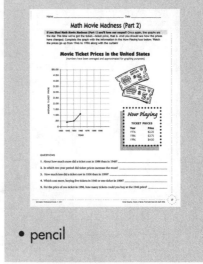

- pencil

## EXTENSION ACTIVITY

Ask students to talk to older relatives or friends about how much they paid to attend the movies when they were young. You also may provide a comparison for students by telling them what movies cost when you were their age. You may even want to talk about double- and triple-feature deals! They can make a similar line graph based on how the price of movies has changed in their short lives. Ask them how they think movie attendance would change if ticket prices were lowered.

# Math Movie Madness (Part 2)

**If you liked Math Movie Madness (Part 1) you'll love our sequel!** Once again, line graphs are the star. This time we've got the ticket—ticket price, that is. And you should see how the prices have changed. Complete the graph with the information in the Now Playing box below. Watch the prices go up from 1946 to 1996 along with the curtain!

## Movie Ticket Prices in the United States
(numbers have been averaged and approximated for graphing purposes)

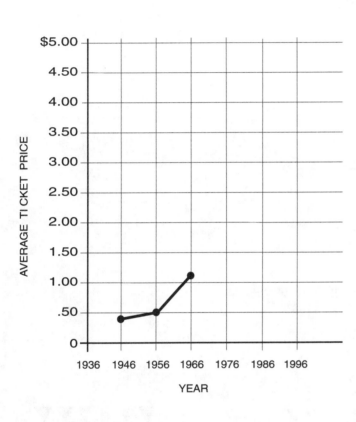

**Now Playing**

### TICKET PRICES

| Year | Price |
|------|-------|
| 1976 | $2.25 |
| 1986 | $3.75 |
| 1996 | $4.50 |

## QUESTIONS

**1.** About how much more did a ticket cost in 1986 than in 1946? _____

**2.** In which ten-year period did ticket prices increase the most? _____

**3.** How much less did a ticket cost in 1956 than in 1996? _____

**4.** Which cost more, buying five tickets in 1946 or one ticket in 1996? _____

**5.** For the price of one ticket in 1996, how many tickets could you buy at the 1946 price? _____

# Math Movie Madness (Part 3)

## Learning Objective

Students use the ideas presented in the last two activities and what they have learned about double bar graphs to understand the relationship between changing ticket prices and movie attendance

### DIRECTIONS

1. Distribute the Math Movie Madness (Part 3) reproducible to students. Explain that they will be using some of the same ideas presented in the previous two activities.

2. Review double bar graphs with students. Remind them that double bar graphs can be used to show and compare total numbers of things, but that each group is divided into two. In this case, the double bar graph will compare how much a movie made at the time it was released to how much the same movie would make based on today's ticket prices.

3. Instruct students to look at the double bar graph and the movie attendance chart, and review the material in the previous activities before answering the questions.

### ANSWERS

**1a.** 75 million   **1b.** 131 million   **1c.** 570 million

**2.** *E.T.*   **3.** *Gone With the Wind*

**4.** 205 million   **5.** 250 million   **6.** 124,135,456

**7.** 100 million   **8.** $0.80

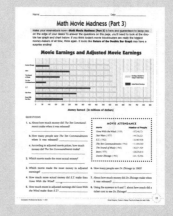

### What You'll Need

- Math Movie Madness (Part 3) reproducible, page 19

- pencil

- two different colored pens or pencils

- calculator

## EXTENSION ACTIVITY

Have students talk about what they think inflation means. Have students go on a grocery store scavenger hunt and get the prices of some everyday items. Then have them do some research in the library about what those items would have cost 5, 10, and 20 years ago. This exercise can be a jumping-off point for essay writing, percents, fraction (of cost), and so forth.

# Math Movie Madness (Part 3)

Make your reservations now—**Math Movie Madness (Part 3)** is here and guaranteed to keep you on the edge of your desks! To answer the questions on this page, you'll need to look at the double bar graph and chart below. If you think today's movie blockbusters are really the biggest money-makers of all time, think again. It looks like this one may have a surprise ending!

## Movie Earnings and Adjusted Movie Earnings

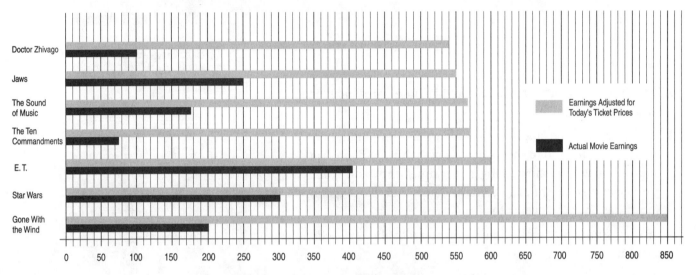

**Money Earned (in millions of dollars)**

## QUESTIONS

**1. a.** About how much money did *The Ten Commandments* make when it was released?

_____

**b.** How many people saw *The Ten Commandments* when it was released? _____

**c.** According to adjusted movie prices, how much money did *The Ten Commandments* make?

_____

**2.** Which movie made the most actual money?

_____

**3.** Which movie made the most money in adjusted earnings? _____

**4.** How much more actual money did *E.T.* make than *Gone With the Wind*? _____

**5.** How much more in adjusted earnings did *Gone With the Wind* make than *E.T.*? _____

### MOVIE ATTENDANCE

| Movie | Number of People |
|---|---|
| *Gone With the Wind* (1939) | 197,548,731 |
| *Star Wars* (1977) | 144,726,521 |
| *E.T.* (1982) | 135,987,938 |
| *The Ten Commandments* (1956) | 131,000,000 |
| *The Sound of Music* (1965) | 130,571,429 |
| *Jaws* (1975) | 128,078,818 |
| *Doctor Zhivago* (1965) | 124,135,456 |

**6.** How many people saw *Dr. Zhivago* in 1965?

_____

**7.** About how much money did *Dr. Zhivago* make when it was released? _____

**8.** Using the answers to 6 and 7, about how much did a ticket cost to see *Dr. Zhivago*? _____

# Sports Graphs Do Double Time

## Learning Objective
Students learn to use double line graphs

### DIRECTIONS

1. Distribute the Sports Graphs Do Double Time reproducible to students.

2. Review double line graphs with students and remind them that line graphs are used to show changes over time. Explain that double line graphs show changes over time for two different groups, in this case boys and girls and how their participation in sports has changed over the years.

3. Instruct students to look at the graph and talk about the changes over time for both groups.

4. Using the information in the Girls Getting in the Game box, students cam complete the graph and then answer the questions.

### ANSWERS

Completed graph should look like this:

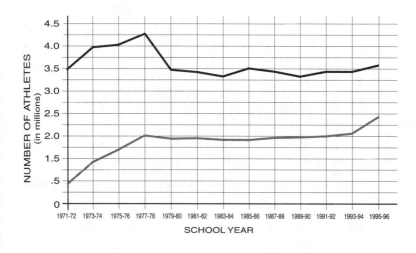

1. girls   2. 1971–72 and 1973–74   3. 1977–78 and 1979–80

4a. 1971–72   4b. 3,100,000   5. 1,200,000

### What You'll Need

- Sports Graphs Do Double Time reproducible, page 21

- pencil

- two different colored pens or pencils

## EXTENSION ACTIVITY

This activity presents an ideal opportunity for essay writing or speaking activities. Ask students why they think the numbers have changed the way that they have over time. Ask students to predict where those numbers will go in the future. As a current events activity, have students look for newspaper clippings or other information on Title IX.

# Sports Graphs Do Double Time

**Let's play!** Today, kids all over the country play many different sports. Check out our graph to see how the number of participants changed between 1971 and 1996. We've given you some numbers to fill in so have those colored pencils ready! Complete the graph by using the information in the box at the bottom of the page. Then answer the questions.

## Participation in U.S. High School Athletics

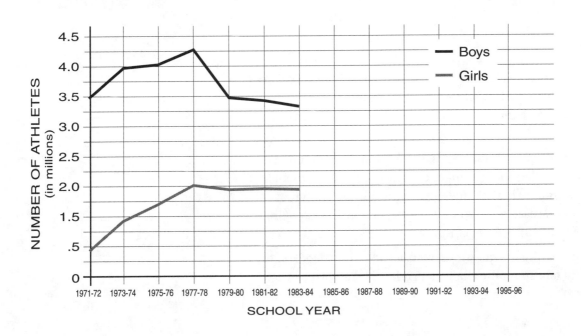

## QUESTIONS

1. Which group experienced the greatest increase from 1971 to 1996? _____

2. Between which two points on the graph did girls' participation increase the most? _____

3. Between which two points on the graph did boys' participation decrease the most? _____

4. **a.** In which year was the difference in the number of girl participants and boy participants the greatest? _____

   **b.** How much was the difference? _____
   _____

5. In 1995–96, about how many more boys participated in sports than girls? _____

| GIRLS GETTING IN THE GAME | | |
|---|---|---|
| | **Boys** | **Girls** |
| 1971–72 | 3,500,000 | 400,000 |
| 1973–74 | just under 4,000,000 | 1,400,000 |
| 1975–76 | just over 4,000,000 | 1,700,000 |
| 1977–78 | 4,250,000 | 2,000,000 |
| 1979–80 | 3,500,000 | 1,800,000 |
| 1981–82 | 3,400,000 | 1,900,00 |
| 1983–84 | 3,300,000 | 1,800,000 |
| 1985–86 | 3,500,000 | 1,800,000 |
| 1987–88 | 3,400,000 | 1,900,000 |
| 1989–90 | 3,300,000 | 1,900,000 |
| 1991–92 | 3,450,000 | 2,000,000 |
| 1993–94 | 3,450,000 | 2,100,000 |
| 1995–96 | 3,600,000 | 2,400,000 |

Scholastic Professional Books • 2001                    *Great Graphs, Charts & Tables That Build Real-Life Math Skills*

# Smoking Stats

## Learning Objective

**Students learn to use triple line graphs**

### What You'll Need

- Smoking Stats reproducible, page 23

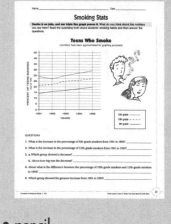

- pencil

### DIRECTIONS

1. Distribute the Smoking Stats reproducible to students. Explain that they will be reading information presented in a triple line graph to compare the number of students who smoke in different grades.

2. Review line graphs with students and remind them that line graphs are used to show changes over time. Explain to them that triple line graphs show changes over time for three different groups. In this case the graph is used to compare the smoking habits of 8th-, 10th-, and 12th-grade students.

3. Before answering the questions, instruct students to look at the graph and talk about the changes that have taken place over time for all three groups.

### ANSWERS

**1.** about 5%    **2.** about 5%    **3a.** 12th graders    **3b.** about 2%

**4.** about 6%    **5.** 10th graders

## EXTENSION ACTIVITY

This activity is great for starting off a group discussion
on a very important topic. It ties in easily with current
events, health and science classes, and is a good opportunity
for students to offer oral or written comments about kids and smoking.
There are a number of statistics available from the American Heart Association,
The Center for Tobacco-Free Kids, and many others.
Have students gather statistics for their state and create a line graph
for the grades at their school or schools in their community.
Post it in the halls or the cafeteria.

# Smoking Stats

**Smoke is no joke, and our triple line graph proves it.** What do you think about the numbers you see here? Read the surprising truth about students' smoking habits and then answer the questions.

## Teens Who Smoke
(numbers have been approximated for graphing purposes)

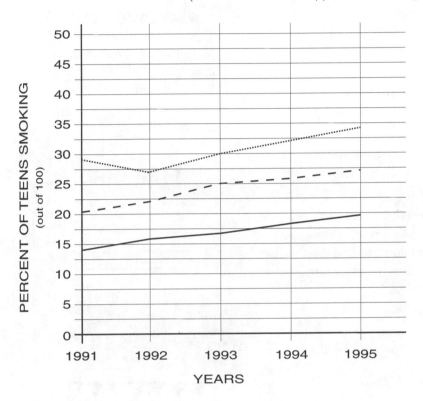

12th grade ·············
10th grade – – – –
8th grade ————

QUESTIONS

**1.** What is the increase in the percentage of 8th-grade smokers from 1991 to 1995? _____

**2.** What is the increase in the percentage of 12th-grade smokers from 1991 to 1995? _____

**3. a.** Which group showed a decrease? _____

    **b.** About how big was the decrease? _____

**4.** About what is the difference between the percentage of 10th-grade smokers and 12th-grade smokers in 1994? _____

**5.** Which group showed the greatest increase from 1991 to 1995? _____

# Math Mileage

## Learning Objective

Students learn to read mileage tables

### What You'll Need

- Math Mileage reproducible, page 25

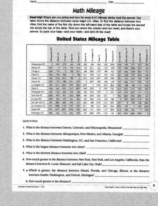

- pencil
- ruler (if necessary)

### DIRECTIONS

1. Distribute the Math Mileage reproducible to students. Explain that they will be reading a mileage table showing the distance between major cities in the United States.

2. Review table reading with students. Explain to them that it requires reading down and across at the same time. Explain the difference between a column and a row.

3. Do an example for the students. Show them how they can use a ruler to keep the columns and rows straight. Also show students how they can drag their fingers across and down to find the intersection of the column and row that holds the answer to their mileage question.

### ANSWERS

1. 920 miles   2. 1407 miles   3. 2840 miles   4. 2946 miles

5. 237 miles   6. 1497 miles   7a. Seattle and Detroit

7b. 982 miles

## EXTENSION ACTIVITIES

Point out to students that the cities listed are the same on both sides of the table. Ask them if it works "both ways" to check the distance between any two cities. Ask students to choose several locations close or far away from the town in which you're located and make a local mileage table. As a cultural or map exercise, ask students to make a mileage table showing the distances between major cities in South America, Africa, Asia, Australia, or Europe.

# Math Mileage

**Road trip!** Where are you going and how far away is it? Mileage tables hold the answer. Our table shows the distance between some major U.S. cities. To find the distance between two cities, find the name of the first city down the left-hand side of the table and locate the second city across the top of the table. Find out where the column and row meet, and there's your answer. So pack your bags—and your math—and let's hit the road!

## United States Mileage Table

| | Albuquerque NM | Atlanta GA | Chicago IL | Dallas TX | Denver CO | Detroit MI | Los Angeles CA | Miami FL | Minneapolis MN | New York NY | St. Louis MO | Salt Lake City UT | San Francisco CA | Seattle WA | Washington, DC |
|---|---|---|---|---|---|---|---|---|---|---|---|---|---|---|---|
| Albuquerque NM | 0 | 1407 | 1335 | 646 | 439 | 1585 | 804 | 1963 | 1222 | 2020 | 1038 | 604 | 1101 | 1433 | 1885 |
| Atlanta GA | 1407 | 0 | 716 | 792 | 1416 | 732 | 2211 | 661 | 1132 | 870 | 555 | 1882 | 2508 | 2673 | 632 |
| Chicago IL | 1335 | 716 | 0 | 928 | 1011 | 286 | 2034 | 1377 | 409 | 821 | 297 | 1403 | 2148 | 2072 | 715 |
| Dallas TX | 646 | 792 | 928 | 0 | 780 | 1211 | 1447 | 1317 | 934 | 1565 | 631 | 1240 | 1747 | 2078 | 1326 |
| Denver CO | 439 | 1416 | 1011 | 780 | 0 | 1274 | 1023 | 2077 | 920 | 1809 | 861 | 512 | 1257 | 1303 | 1700 |
| Detroit MI | 1585 | 732 | 286 | 1211 | 1274 | 0 | 2297 | 1389 | 696 | 640 | 547 | 1666 | 2411 | 2359 | 534 |
| Los Angeles CA | 804 | 2211 | 2034 | 1447 | 1023 | 2297 | 0 | 2752 | 1943 | 2824 | 1842 | 688 | 380 | 1151 | 2689 |
| Miami FL | 1963 | 661 | 1377 | 1317 | 2077 | 1389 | 2752 | 0 | 1793 | 1281 | 1216 | 2543 | 3131 | 1052 | 1043 |
| Minneapolis MN | 1222 | 1132 | 409 | 934 | 920 | 696 | 1943 | 1793 | 0 | 1231 | 619 | 1312 | 2057 | 1117 | 1125 |
| New York NY | 2020 | 870 | 821 | 1565 | 1809 | 640 | 2824 | 1281 | 1231 | 0 | 982 | 2201 | 2946 | 2894 | 237 |
| St. Louis MO | 1038 | 555 | 297 | 631 | 861 | 547 | 1842 | 1216 | 619 | 982 | 0 | 1327 | 2072 | 2118 | 845 |
| Salt Lake City UT | 604 | 1882 | 1403 | 1240 | 512 | 1666 | 688 | 2543 | 1312 | 2201 | 1327 | 0 | 745 | 828 | 2095 |
| San Francisco CA | 1101 | 2508 | 2148 | 1747 | 1257 | 2411 | 380 | 3131 | 2057 | 2946 | 2072 | 745 | 0 | 820 | 2840 |
| Seattle WA | 1433 | 2673 | 2072 | 2078 | 1303 | 2359 | 1151 | 1052 | 1117 | 2894 | 2118 | 828 | 820 | 0 | 2788 |
| Washington, DC | 1885 | 632 | 715 | 1326 | 1700 | 534 | 2689 | 1043 | 1125 | 237 | 845 | 2095 | 2840 | 2788 | 0 |

## QUESTIONS

**1.** What is the distance between Denver, Colorado, and Minneapolis, Minnesota? _____

**2.** What is the distance between Albuquerque, New Mexico, and Atlanta, Georgia? _____

**3.** What is the distance between Washington, DC, and San Francisco, California? _____

**4.** What is the largest distance between two cities? _____

**5.** What is the shortest distance between two cities? _____

**6.** How much greater is the distance between New York, New York, and Los Angeles, California, than the distance between St. Louis, Missouri, and Salt Lake City, Utah?_____

**7. a.** Which is greater, the distance between Miami, Florida, and Chicago, Illinois, or the distance between Seattle, Washington, and Detroit, Michigan? _____

**b.** How much greater is the distance? _____

# Dinosaurs on the Map

## Learning Objective

Students learn to read standard map grids

## DIRECTIONS

1. Distribute the Dinosaurs on the Map reproducible to students. Explain that they will be using map grids to locate dinosaur fossils discovered in the United States.

2. Review mapping with students and explain that the letter-number combination is used to provide directions. Be sure they remember the difference between a column and a row.

3. Instruct students to look at the map while you give an example of how to find locations using the coordinates. Show how students they can use the "drag the finger" method to locate the square where the row and column indicated by the coordinate intersect.

4. Give students a few minutes to familiarize themselves with the map. Then they can use the map index at the bottom of the page to answer the questions.

## ANSWERS

Completed map should look like this:

## What You'll Need

- Dinosaurs on the Map reproducible, page 27

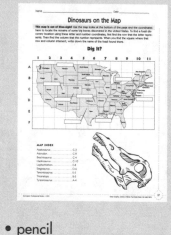

- pencil

## EXTENSION ACTIVITIES

Dinosaurs are a favorite with kids. This activity provides ample opportunity for crossover teaching in science. Have students write reports on the dinosaurs they've located on the map. Students can do a little archaeology research on the World Wide Web or in the library, and find the location of even more dinosaur fossil discoveries to map on their own or as a group. This also can be done with fossils or other archaeological discoveries in different parts of the world for a more challenging and culturally stimulating mapping exercise. If a nearby museum has any dinosaur fossils on display, there is likely a map there. A field trip could be mathematically and scientifically beneficial.

# Dinosaurs on the Map

**This map is out of dino-sight!** Use the map index at the bottom of the page and the coordinates here to locate the remains of some big bones discovered in the United States. To find a fossil discovery location using these letter and number coordinates, first find the row that the letter represents. Then find the column that the number represents. When you find the square where that row and column intersect, write down the name of the fossil found there.

## Dig It?

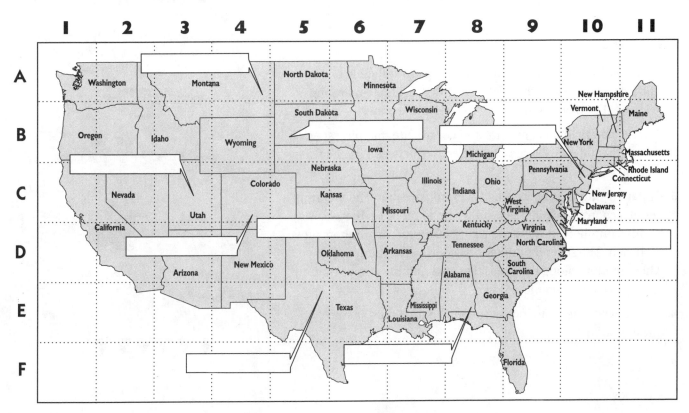

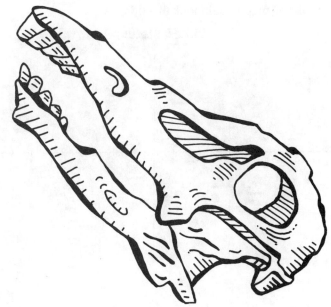

**MAP INDEX**

| | |
|---|---|
| Apatosaurus | C-3 |
| Astrodon | C-9 |
| Brachiosaurus | C-4 |
| Hadrosaurus | C-10 |
| Lophorhothon | E-8 |
| Stegosaurus | D-6 |
| Tenontosaurus | E-5 |
| Triceratops | B-5 |
| Tyrannosaurus | A-4 |

# Coordinate Math Mapping

## Learning Objective

Students work with coordinate mapping

### DIRECTIONS

1. Distribute the Coordinate Math Mapping reproducible to students. Explain that they will be using coordinate mapping to locate the wackiest museums in the United States.

2. Review map reading in general and coordinate mapping specifically with students. Discuss the difference between the $x$-axis and the $y$-axis.

3. Explain to students how to read a coordinate pair. The first number of a coordinate pair tells you where to move on the $x$-axis. Positive numbers move to the right of 0, negative numbers move to the left. The second number of a coordinate pair tells you where to move along the $y$-axis. Positive numbers move up from 0, negative numbers move down.

4. Encourage students to look at the map before they answer questions.

### ANSWERS

Completed map should look like this:

### What You'll Need

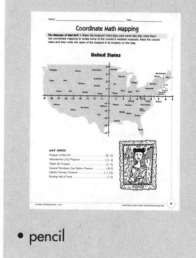

- Coordinate Math Mapping reproducible, page 29

- pencil

### EXTENSION ACTIVITY

Have students create a list of interesting places they've visited nearby or far away, such as parks, museums, cities, and restaurants. Ask students to locate these places on a map or create their own map. They then can assign coordinates to the various locations, swap maps with a classmate, and send each other on a "trip" to locate the sites.

# Coordinate Math Mapping

**The Museum of Bad Art?** A Water Ski Museum? Field trips were never like this, were they? Use coordinate mapping to locate some of the country's wackiest museums. Read the coordinates and then write the name of the museum in its location on the map.

## United States

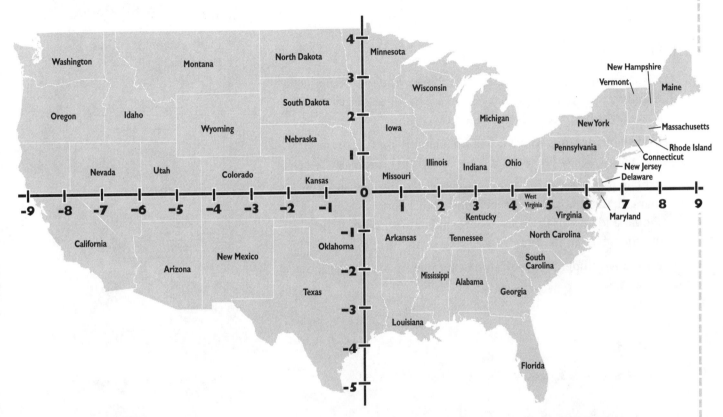

### MAP INDEX

Museum of Bad Art . . . . . . . . . . . . . . . . . . . . . . . . . . . (8, 1.5)

International U.F.O. Museum . . . . . . . . . . . . . . . . . (–3, –2)

Water Ski Museum . . . . . . . . . . . . . . . . . . . . . . . . . (5, –5)

General Petroleum Gas Station Museum . . . . . . . . (–8, 4)

Dakota Dinosaur Museum . . . . . . . . . . . . . . . . . . (–1, 3.5)

Bowling Hall of Fame . . . . . . . . . . . . . . . . . . . . . . (1, 0)

Scholastic Professional Books • 2001   Great Graphs, Charts & Tables That Build Real-Life Math Skills

# Picto-Players

## Learning Objective

Students learn to use pictographs

### What You'll Need

- Picto-Players reproducible, page 31

- pencil

- scratch paper or calculator

## DIRECTIONS

1. Distribute the Picto-Players reproducible to students. Explain that they will be using pictographs to answer questions about some favorite sports kids their age like to play.

2. Review pictographs with students, explaining that pictographs use pictures or symbols to represent a certain number of things.

3. Explain to students that when answering questions using a pictograph, they should count the number of symbols. Then they should add up—or multiply—that number according to the number given in the key.

4. Encourage students to look at the chart before answering the questions.

## ANSWERS

**1.** 40   **2.** soccer   **3.** gymnastics   **4.** 155   **5.** 340   **6.** 34

## EXTENSION ACTIVITIES

Students can have lots of fun devising their own pictographs, which can be used to show numbers of a variety of things. For example, if your school has an end-of-the-year picnic, students can find out how many hamburgers, hot dogs, bags of chips, and so forth, will be provided, then create pictographs to represent those numbers. Symbols also may be "stacked" as if they were on a graph. Have students rearrange the pictograph given so the categories (such as baseball) run across the bottom of the graph and the symbols are stacked vertically above each category. As an art extension, have students create their own symbols.

# Picto-Players

**Can you picture what kind of sports you might want to play after school today or over this weekend?** Can you picto-graph it? Now you can, with our pictograph that shows the favorite sports of kids just like you. How many kids like to play what? Add it up using our key and answer the questions.

## Top Five Favorite Sports to Play

 = 10 kids          = 5 kids

| | |
|---|---|
| **Baseball** | 🏃🏃🏃🏃🏃🏃🏃🏃🏃🏃🏃🏃🏃🏃 |
| **Basketball** | 🏃🏃🏃🏃🏃🏃🏃🏃🏃🏃🏃🏃 |
| **Football** | 🏃🏃🏃🏃🏃🏃🏃🏃🏃🏃🏃🏃🏃 |
| **Gymnastics** | 🏃🏃🏃 |
| **Soccer** | 🏃🏃🏃🏃🏃🏃🏃🏃🏃🏃🏃🏃🏃🏃🏃🏃🏃🏃🏃 |

### QUESTIONS

**1.** Gymnastics is the favorite sport of how many kids? _____

**2.** Which sport is the favorite of the most kids? _____

**3.** Which sport is the favorite of the fewest kids? _____

**4.** How many kids say basketball is their favorite sport to play? _____

**5.** If you add the number kids who say football is their favorite sport to the number of kids who say baseball is their favorite sport, what number do you get? _____

**6.** How many pictures would represent the answer you got in question 5? _____

Scholastic Professional Books • 2001          Great Graphs, Charts & Tables That Build Real-Life Math Skills

# Shopping for Math

## Learning Objective

Students learn to read for detail using food labels

### DIRECTIONS

1. Distribute the Shopping for Math reproducible to students. Explain that they will be reading for detail by looking at food labels.

2. Talk about food labels with students. Before they look at the reproducible, have the class brainstorm the kinds of information they think can be found on food labels. Ask them if they ever look at food labels at home or in the grocery store.

3. Instruct students to answer the questions.

### ANSWERS

1. 242  2. 35  3. 25  4. 30%  5. 3  6. 12%  7. about 260  8. 14

### ▲▲▲▲▲▲▲
## What You'll Need

- Shopping for Math reproducible, page 33

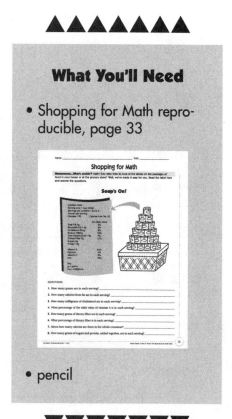

- pencil

▼▼▼▼▼▼

## EXTENSION ACTIVITIES

Students can bring food labels from home and compare the statistics they find there. To extend this activity to much larger amounts, labels from bulk food packaging could be obtained from the cafeteria. The percentage of daily value statistic can help teach percents, fractions, and decimals. The serving size is often a fraction; asking students to find the total amount of food in a package can be a way to teach multiplying fractions. Servings are often given in grams as well, and present an ideal way to talk about metrics and do some basic conversions. The nutritive values of various foods can be a good discussion for science or health class.

Name _____ Date _____

# Shopping for Math

**Mmmmmmm...What's cookin'?** Math! Ever take time to look at the labels on the packages of food in your house or at the grocery store? Well, we've made it easy for you. Read the label here and answer the questions.

## Soup's On!

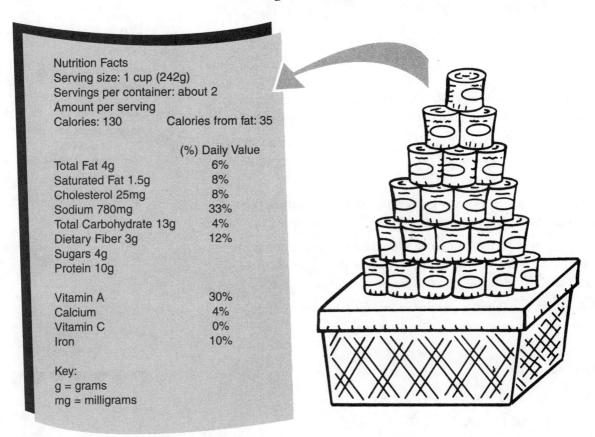

Nutrition Facts
Serving size: 1 cup (242g)
Servings per container: about 2
Amount per serving
Calories: 130          Calories from fat: 35

|                          | (%) Daily Value |
|--------------------------|-----------------|
| Total Fat 4g             | 6%              |
| Saturated Fat 1.5g       | 8%              |
| Cholesterol 25mg         | 8%              |
| Sodium 780mg             | 33%             |
| Total Carbohydrate 13g   | 4%              |
| Dietary Fiber 3g         | 12%             |
| Sugars 4g                |                 |
| Protein 10g              |                 |
|                          |                 |
| Vitamin A                | 30%             |
| Calcium                  | 4%              |
| Vitamin C                | 0%              |
| Iron                     | 10%             |

Key:
g = grams
mg = milligrams

## QUESTIONS

**1.** How many grams are in each serving? _____

**2.** How many calories from fat are in each serving? _____

**3.** How many milligrams of cholesterol are in each serving? _____

**4.** What percentage of the daily value of vitamin A is in each serving? _____

**5.** How many grams of dietary fiber are in each serving? _____

**6.** What percentage of dietary fiber is in each serving? _____

**7.** About how many calories are there in the whole container? _____

**8.** How many grams of sugars and protein, added together, are in each serving? _____

Scholastic Professional Books • 2001          Great Graphs, Charts & Tables That Build Real-Life Math Skills

# Math-in-a-Box

## Learning Objective
Students learn to read box scores

### DIRECTIONS

1. Distribute the Math-in-a-Box reproducible to students. Explain that they will be reading for detail by looking at a box score.

2. Review chart reading with students and remind them that when a lot of information is being presented, many of the important statistics may be abbreviated.

3. Go over the box score on page 35 with students and draw their attention to the key that explains the abbreviations used.

4. It is very important to remind students that they do not have to understand what a particular item is—free throw, for example—to be able to locate the information on the chart.

5. Ask students to familiarize themselves with the chart before answering the questions.

### ANSWERS

**1.** 25    **2.** 12    **3.** 18    **4.** Jordan's total points

**5a.** 2    **5b.** 1    **6a.** 13    **6b.** 4    **7.** 87

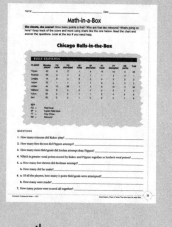

## What You'll Need

- Math-in-a-Box reproducible, page 35

- pencil

## EXTENSION ACTIVITY

Box scores can be found in almost any newspaper on almost any day. Box scores vary for different sports, so there is a wide variety of keys and formats to choose from. Students can bring in box scores from the paper or create ones on their own based on the performance of their own team or teams at school.

# Math-in-a-Box

**She shoots, she scores!** How many points is that? Who got that last rebound? What's going on here? Keep track of the score and more using charts like the one below. Read the chart and answer the questions. Look at the key if you need help.

## Chicago Bulls-in-the-Box

### BULLS STATISTICS

| PLAYER | Minutes played | FG made | FG attempted | 3P made | 3P attempted | FT made | FT attempted | RB points | Total |
|---|---|---|---|---|---|---|---|---|---|
| Pippen | 43 | 6 | 17 | 1 | 4 | 10 | 12 | 9 | 23 |
| Rodman | 33 | 0 | 4 | 0 | 1 | 1 | 2 | 11 | 1 |
| Longley | 14 | 0 | 4 | 0 | 0 | 0 | 0 | 3 | 0 |
| Harper | 18 | 1 | 4 | 0 | 1 | 0 | 0 | 3 | 2 |
| Jordan | 44 | 15 | 35 | 1 | 4 | 8 | 10 | 11 | 39 |
| Williams | 23 | 2 | 5 | 0 | 0 | 0 | 0 | 7 | 4 |
| Kukoc | 25 | 3 | 6 | 1 | 1 | 2 | 4 | 4 | 9 |
| Kerr | 25 | 3 | 5 | 1 | 2 | 2 | 2 | 1 | 9 |

**KEY**

FG = Field Goal

3P = 3-point Field Goal

FT = Free Throw

RB = Rebound

## QUESTIONS

1. How many minutes did Kukoc play? _____

2. How many free throws did Pippen attempt? _____

3. How many more field goals did Jordan attempt than Pippen? _____

4. Which is greater: total points scored by Kukoc and Pippen together or Jordan's total points? _____

5. **a.** How many free throws did Rodman attempt? _____

   **b.** How many did he make? _____

6. **a.** Of all the players, how many 3-point field goals were attempted? _____

   **b.** How many were made? _____

7. How many points were scored all together? _____

# Mutt Math

## Learning Objective
Students read a point chart

### DIRECTIONS

1. Distribute the Mutt Math reproducible to students. Explain that they will be reading for detail by looking at the point chart used to score dogs in a dog show.

2. Review chart reading with students, and remind them that reading the question carefully first can make locating the information they need to answer the question much simpler.

3. Go over the Dog Show Point Chart with students. Explain that M and F stand for male and female, and that the number of points a dog earns in a show depends on the number of dogs competing. The minimum number of male or female dogs that must compete in each point category is listed next to the name of each breed.

4. Do an example with students. For example: A Brittany that wins over eight other male Brittanys, earns three points.

5. Instruct students to familiarize themselves with the chart before answering the questions.

### ANSWERS

1. Chow Chows   2. 2   3. 5   4. 12   5a. 5   5b. 16   6a. 3   6b. 6

## What You'll Need

- Mutt Math reproducible, page 37

- pencil

## EXTENSION ACTIVITIES

The American Kennel Club can provide a great deal of scoring. Have the class watch the Westminster Kennel Club show together and follow along with pad and paper as the show is scored. Find out if any students or their friends have ever shown their dog in competition. There are also cat shows, and researching those scoring techniques provides a completely different set of information and a whole new activity.

# Mutt Math

**These dogs are hardly mutts, but they can still do mutt math.** Can you? Dogs earn points at a show, but how many depends on the number of dogs that show up! Read the chart and answer the questions. The names of the breeds are listed on the left. The number of points a dog can earn in a show is listed across the top. For a dog to earn the number of points you see listed, at least that many male (M) or female (F) dogs must have competed.

## Dog Show Point Chart

| Breed | 1 pt. | | 2 pts. | | 3 pts. | | 4 pts. | | 5 pts. | |
|-------|---|---|---|---|----|----|----|----|----|----|
| | M | F | M | F | M | F | M | F | M | F |
| Brittanys | 2 | 2 | 4 | 6 | 7 | 10 | 10 | 16 | 16 | 26 |
| Pointers | 2 | 2 | 3 | 3 | 5 | 5 | 6 | 6 | 8 | 9 |
| Collies | 2 | 2 | 6 | 7 | 11 | 13 | 19 | 21 | 34 | 36 |
| Huskies | 3 | 3 | 8 | 11 | 14 | 20 | 20 | 28 | 31 | 43 |
| St. Bernards | 2 | 2 | 4 | 4 | 7 | 7 | 10 | 11 | 16 | 17 |
| Chow Chows | 2 | 2 | 4 | 4 | 6 | 6 | 7 | 7 | 9 | 9 |

QUESTIONS

1. Which breed has the same point requirements for male and female dogs? _____

2. If a female Brittany wins a show and there are five other female Brittanys in the show, how many points does the dog earn? _____

3. How many points does a female Chow Chow earn if she wins against eight other females? _____

4. How many more female Huskies than male have to compete for a dog to win five points? _____

5. **a.** A female St. Bernard wins against 16 other females. How many points does she win? _____

   **b.** How many males would have to compete for the dog to earn that number of points? _____

6. **a.** How many more male Collies than Pointers are required to compete for a dog to earn two points? _____     **b.** Three points? _____

Great Graphs, Charts & Tables That Build Real-Life Math Skills

# Tune In to Schedules

## Learning Objective
Students work with on-air time schedules

▲▲▲▲▲▲▲

### What You'll Need

- Tune In to Schedules reproducible, page 39

- pencil

▼▼▼▼▼▼

### DIRECTIONS

1. Distribute the Tune In to Schedules reproducible to students. Explain that they will be reading for detail using a time schedule from a radio station.

2. Review time with students, and remind them that this schedule repeats every hour, which is why they do not see any numbers in the "hour" column. They will only see numbers that represent minutes past the hour.

3. Look over the schedule with students and answer any questions. Discuss the definitions of station I.D., testimonial, Public Service Announcement, C-Note that are found in the key.

4. Instruct students to look over the schedule and the key, before they answer the questions.

### ANSWERS

**1.** 15  **2.** 27  **3.** 1  **4.** 18  **5.** 12

## EXTENSION ACTIVITIES

A visit to a local radio station or an in-class visit from a local radio personality could be a fun way to enhance this math activity. If a trip or visit isn't possible, a local radio or television station would very likely fax you their schedule to use in class. Schedules often vary depending on the time of day or day of week, so a wide variety of activities is possible.

Name _____ Date _____

# Tune In to Schedules

**Math is hitting the airwaves with some serious scheduling!** Read the following hour clock used by a radio station to keep track of songs, weather, and all sorts of stuff! The key below explains the abbreviations we've used. Remember that this schedule repeats every hour.

## Radio Time

**Hour Clock for 8:00 A.M. to 2:00 P.M.** (schedule repeats every hour)

| | |
|---|---|
| :00 | Station I.D. |
| :01 | Three songs |
| :12 | Station I.D. |
| :13 | Song |
| :15 | Station I.D. |
| :16 | Song |
| :18 | Weather and PSA |
| :19 | Song |
| :23 | Station I.D. |
| :24 | Song |
| :27 | Testimonial |
| :28 | Song |
| :30 | Station I.D. |
| :31 | Song |
| :34 | Station I.D. |
| :35 | Song |
| :38 | Station I.D. |
| :39 | Song |
| :42 | Station I.D. |
| :43 | Song |
| :46 | C-Note |
| :47 | Song |
| :50 | Testimonial |
| :51 | Song |
| :54 | Station I.D. |
| :55 | Song |
| :58 | 2-minute news brief |

### QUESTIONS

**1.** How many songs are played each hour? _____

**2.** How many minutes past the hour is the first testimonial? _____

**3.** How many public service announcements are there each hour? _____

**4.** After the first station I.D., about how many minutes until the weather is reported? _____

**5.** How many minutes are between the C-note and the news brief? _____

## KEY

**Station I.D.:** Tells listeners the station they're listening to

**C-Note:** Information about an upcoming event

**PSA:** Public Service Announcement

**Testimonial:** Recording of a listener talking about why he or she likes the station

*Scholastic Professional Books • 2001*                    *Great Graphs, Charts & Tables That Build Real-Life Math Skills*

# Circle Survey

## Learning Objective

Students learn to use circle or "pie" graphs

### DIRECTIONS

1. Distribute the Circle Survey reproducible to students. Explain that they will be reading and interpreting a circle graph showing the results of a survey taken by kids just like them about issues facing the United States.

2. Review circle graphs with students and explain that they are used to show parts of a whole. Like cutting a pie into pieces, students can look at the size of each piece to understand statistical information. The pie represents the views of all kids surveyed, each piece represents the percentage of kids surveyed who feel that particular issue is most important.

3. Instruct students to look at the graph and talk about the results. You may wish to briefly discuss percents so that students are not confused about what they are seeing.

4. Instruct students to answer the questions based on the information given.

### ANSWERS

**1.** 36%   **2.** 40%   **3.** 71%   **4.** 53%   **5.** 100%

**6.** 24%   **7.** 36 kids   **8.** Answers will vary

## What You'll Need

- Circle Survey reproducible, page 41

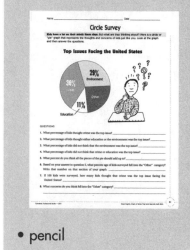

- pencil

## EXTENSION ACTIVITIES

Depending on the students' level, percents can be discussed in more detail. For an even more challenging exercise, the percents can be written as fractions or decimals. The issues raised by this survey can lead into a larger discussion that works well in a current events class or as an essay-writing exercise or homework assignment. Ask students what they think fell into the "Other" category. (The topics included AIDS, abortion, prejudice/racism, violence, and drug and alcohol abuse.) Conduct a similar survey in your class, grade, or school and graph the results. Do students think their concerns are different than the concerns of adults?

Name _____  Date _____

# Circle Survey

**Kids have a lot on their minds these days.** But what are they thinking about? Here is a circle or "pie" graph that represents the thoughts and concerns of kids just like you. Look at the graph and then answer the questions.

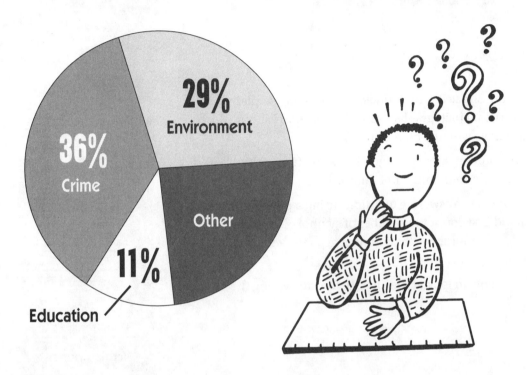

## Top Issues Facing the United States

QUESTIONS

**1.** What percentage of kids thought crime was the top issue? _____

**2.** What percentage of kids thought either education or the environment was the top issue? _____

**3.** What percentage of kids did not think that the environment was the top issue? _____

**4.** What percentage of kids did not think that crime or education was the top issue? _____

**5.** What percent do you think all the pieces of the pie should add up to? _____

**6.** Based on your answer to question 5, what percent age of kids surveyed fell into the "Other" category? Write that number on that section of your graph. _____

**7.** If 100 kids were surveyed, how many kids thought that crime was the top issue facing the United States? _____

**8.** What concerns do you think fell into the "Other" category? _____

_____

Scholastic Professional Books • 2001

Great Graphs, Charts & Tables That Build Real-Life Math Skills

# Super Pix!

## Learning Objective

**Students read pictographs**

### What You'll Need

• Super Pix! reproducible, page 43

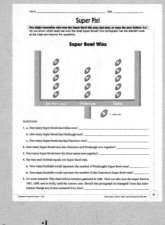

• pencil

• scratch paper

## DIRECTIONS

1. Distribute the Super Pix! reproducible to students. Explain that they will be using pictographs to answer questions about which NFL teams have won the most Super Bowls.

2. Review with students that pictographs use pictures or symbols to represent a certain number of things.

3. Explain that when answering questions using a pictograph, students should first count the number of symbols. Then they should add—or multiply—that number according to the number given in the key.

4. Instruct students to look at the chart before answering the questions.

## ANSWERS

**1a.** 5    **1b.** 4    **1c.** 5    **2.** 9    **3.** 14

**4a.** 2    **4b.** 2 1/2    **5.** Answers may vary

## EXTENSION ACTIVITIES

This activity can be changed by designating a different value for each symbol (as done in question 4). Students can have lots of fun devising their own pictographs, which can be used to show numbers of a variety of things. For example, if your school library has a book drive, a chart could be made to keep track of the number of books collected. For example, each book can represent every 10 books that are collected. Or students can come up with an entirely different symbol.

Symbols do not necessarily need to be stacked in graph form as they are here. Have students rearrange the pictograph so that the team names are listed and the footballs are to the right of each team name. As an art extension, have students design their own symbols. Ask students if they can combine pictographs with another type of graph, for example, a circle graph.

# Super Pix!

**You might remember who won the Super Bowl this year, last year, or even the year before.** But do you know which team has won the most Super Bowls? Our pictograph has the answer! Look at the chart and answer the questions.

## Super Bowl Wins

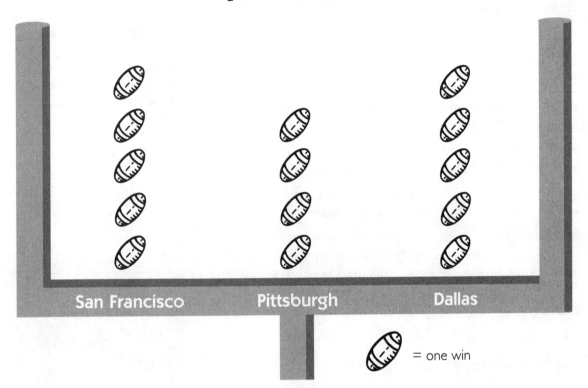

= one win

QUESTIONS

**1. a.** How many Super Bowls has Dallas won? _____

   **b.** How many Super Bowls has Pittsburgh won? _____

   **c.** How many Super Bowls has San Francisco won? _____

**2.** How many Super Bowls have San Francisco and Pittsburgh won together? _____

**3.** How many Super Bowls have the three teams won together? _____

**4.** Say that each football equals two Super Bowl wins.

   **a.** How many footballs would represent the number of Pittsburgh's Super Bowl wins? _____

   **b.** How many footballs would represent the number of San Francisco's Super Bowl wins? _____

**5.** Do some research: This chart is from statistics gathered in 1996.  Find out who won the Super Bowl in 1997, 1998, and so forth, until the current year. Should this pictograph be changed? Does this information change any of your answers? If so, how? _____

Scholastic Professional Books • 2001                    Great Graphs, Charts & Tables That Build Real-Life Math Skills

# Today's Forecast: Maps!

## Learning Objective
Students read a weather map

### DIRECTIONS

1. Distribute the Today's Forecast: Maps! reproducible to students. It may look familiar to many of them.

2. Review the map legend with the students. In particular, go over the meanings of the abbreviations listed in the legend.

3. Explain to students that the two numbers listed near each city name refer to that day's high and low temperature.

4. There is a lot of information being presented here, so remind students to read questions carefully. This will help them look for the right information and use their time wisely and efficiently.

### ANSWERS

**1.** 66    **2.** 56    **3.** Answers will vary    **4.** 49 degrees

**5.** 13 degrees    **6.** Fairbanks, Alaska

**7.** Key West, Florida

**8.** Answers will vary

## What You'll Need

- Today's Forecast: Maps! reproducible, page 45

- pencil

- paper

## EXTENSION ACTIVITIES

This is an activity that can change every day. Weather maps often are accompanied by charts listing everything from historical highs and lows to rainfall and tides. The weather maps shown on the television news may present different information, more specifically tailored to your town. Researching the local weather news can make an ideal take-home assignment. Have students design other pictographs, for example, to go along with the weather map. For example, one raindrop could equal an inch of precipitation. Also, temperatures presented here are in degrees Fahrenheit. Discuss Celsius and when and where it's used. For more challenging math, have students convert temperatures.

# Today's Forecast: Maps!

**Before you get on that plane, you'd better check the weather so you know what to pack!**

Don't worry—you don't have to be a meteorologist. You just need our weather map. Look at the chart and answer the questions.

## Chart the Weather

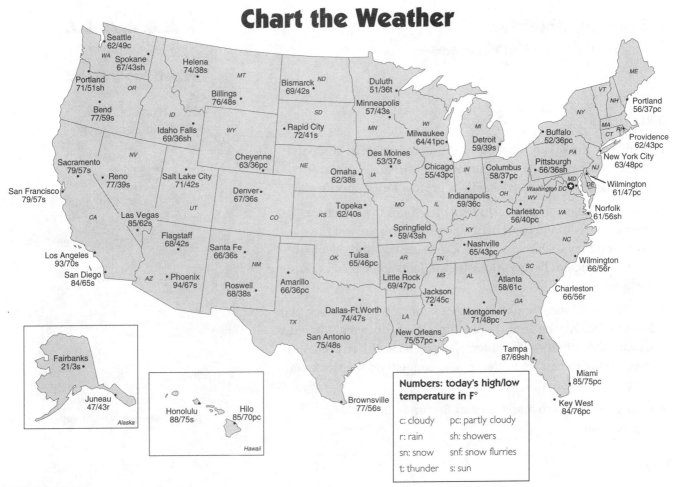

**Numbers: today's high/low temperature in F°**

c: cloudy    pc: partly cloudy

r: rain    sh: showers

sn: snow    snf: snow flurries

t: thunder    s: sun

## QUESTIONS

1. What was the high temperature in Santa Fe, New Mexico? _____

2. What was the low temperature in Wilmington, North Carolina? _____

3. Name three cities with partly cloudy skies. _____

4. How much greater was the low temperature in Los Angeles, California, than the high temperature in Fairbanks, Alaska? _____

5. What was the difference between the low and high temperatures in Honolulu, Hawaii? _____

6. Which city had the lowest high temperature? _____

7. Which city had the highest low temperature? _____

8. Name cities in four different states with showers. _____

# Taking Stock of Stocks

## Learning Objective

Students learn to read basic stock charts

▲▲▲▲▲▲▲

**What You'll Need**

- Taking Stock of Stocks reproducible, page 47

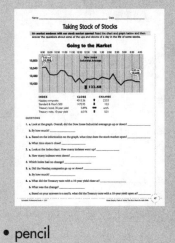

- pencil

▼▼▼▼▼▼▼

## DIRECTIONS

1. Distribute the Taking Stock of Stocks reproducible to students. Explain that they will be reading some basic stock quotes from the newspaper showing the activity of stocks on a specific day.

2. Review chart reading with students. Tell them to familiarize themselves with the chart before attempting to answer the questions. You may wish to discuss stocks in general and the chart here in particular before asking the students to begin answering the questions.

3. It is likely that most students are not familiar with the stock market and this may be a source of intimidation for them. When discussing the activity with students, it may be useful to point out that it is not necessary to completely understand the stock market to do this activity.

4. Instruct students to read the chart first and then answer the questions.

## ANSWERS

**1a.** down   **1b.** 122.68   **2a.** 9:30 A.M.   **2b.** 4:00 P.M.

**3a.** 2   **3b.** 1   **4.** Treasury bond, 30-year yield

**5a.** up   **5b.** 23.53   **6a.** 6.01%   **6b.** 0.01   **6c.** 6.00%

## EXTENSION ACTIVITIES

There are stock quotes in the paper every day that can be used for classroom activities, in addition to a number of Web sites (see page 59) that provide constant updates. The example given here is a very simplified version, but actual stock quotes provide fractions, decimals, sometimes percents—they are a gold mine of statistics.

As an ongoing project, it can be fun and educational to have the class track some stocks over time. Allow the kids to choose the stocks themselves (there are many that would be popular with kids, including some clothing and shoe designers, fast-food chains, and entertainment groups) and chart the stocks on a giant line graph in your classroom or hallway.

# Taking Stock of Stocks

**It's market madness with our stock market quotes!** Read the chart and graph below and then answer the questions about some of the ups and downs of a day in the life of some stocks.

## Going to the Market

| INDEX | CLOSE | | CHANGE |
| --- | --- | --- | --- |
| Nasdaq composite | 4013.36 | ⬆ | 23.53 |
| Standard & Poor's 500 | 1475.95 | ⬇ | 10.5 |
| Treasury bond, 30-year yield | 5.89% | ⬌ | unch. |
| Treasury note, 10-year yield | 6.01% | ⬆ | 0.01 |

## QUESTIONS

**1. a.** Look at the graph. Overall, did the Dow Jones Industrial average go up or down? _____

  **b.** By how much? _____

**2. a.** Based on the information on the graph, what time does the stock market open? _____

  **b.** What time does it close? _____

**3. a.** Look at the Index chart. How many indexes went up? _____

  **b.** How many indexes went down? _____

**4.** Which index had no change? _____

**5. a.** Did the Nasdaq composite go up or down? _____

  **b.** By how much? _____

**6. a.** What did the Treasury note with a 10-year yield close at? _____

  **b.** What was the change? _____

  **c.** Based on your answers to a and b, what did the Treasury note with a 10-year yield open at? _____

# Dinner Diagrams

## Learning Objective

Students create Venn diagrams

## DIRECTIONS

1. Distribute the Dinner Diagrams reproducible to students.

2. Review Venn diagrams with students and make sure that they understand what a Venn diagram is used to represent. Compare a Venn diagram to other graphs and discuss how the Venn diagram is different.

3. Mention to students that Venn diagrams represent what two or more different groups have in common. Mention that a Venn diagram represents an "overlap" of groups, just as they see the circles themselves overlap.

4. Have a brief discussion about possible situations—aside from what is presented in the activity—for which a Venn diagram might be used.

5. Instruct students to draw Venn diagrams to represent the requested information.

## What You'll Need

- Dinner Diagrams reproducible, page 49

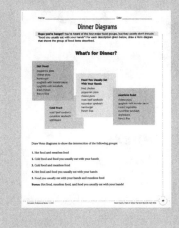

- pencil

- protractor for drawing circles (optional)

## ANSWERS

1.

4.

2.

5.

3.

Bonus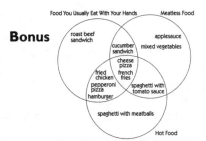

## EXTENSION ACTIVITIES

Have students create a similar set of Venn diagrams based on the food that they find in their school cafeteria. Encourage them to be as creative as possible with the groups that they decide to create. They may use colors, textures, ingredients—anything that can be classified as a group. And of course, challenge students to create Venn diagrams of items other than food. They may want to try sporting equipment—such as items used with hands, feet, or heads. Students can also create "Venn collages" in which pictures are used to illustrate grouped items as opposed to words or numbers.

# Dinner Diagrams

**Hope you're hungry!** You've heard of the four major food groups, but they usually don't include "food you usually eat with your hands"! For each description given below, draw a Venn diagram that shows the group of food items described.

## What's for Dinner?

**Hot Food**

pepperoni pizza
cheese pizza
hamburger
spaghetti with tomato sauce
spaghetti with meatballs
fried chicken
french fries

**Food You Usually Eat With Your Hands**

fried chicken
pepperoni pizza
cheese pizza
roast beef sandwich
cucumber sandwich
hamburger
french fries

**Cold Food**

roast beef sandwich
cucumber sandwich
applesauce

**Meatless Food**

cheese pizza
spaghetti with tomato sauce
mixed vegetables
cucumber sandwich
applesauce
french fries

Draw Venn diagrams to show the intersection of the following groups:

**1.** Hot food and meatless food

**2.** Cold food and food you usually eat with your hands

**3.** Cold food and meatless food

**4.** Hot food and food you usually eat with your hands

**5.** Food you usually eat with your hands and meatless food

**Bonus:** Hot food, meatless food, and food you usually eat with your hands!

# Menu Math

## Learning Objective

Students read a menu

### DIRECTIONS

1. Distribute the Menu Math reproducible to students.

2. Review the basics of money math with students, such as adding and subtracting with decimals. Make sure students are comfortable with regrouping when adding and subtracting decimals.

3. Instruct students to do the calculations by hand. Later, if you wish, they may check their work—or their neighbor's work—with a calculator.

4. For many students, decimals are not as "scary" when used in a money context, something that they are familiar with. Illustrating the use of decimals as a means of counting money can help make students more comfortable with decimals in general.

5. Before they attempt to answer the questions, explain to students the difference between ordering a dinner or ordering a la carte.

6. Students can then answer the questions.

## What You'll Need

- Menu Math reproducible, page 51

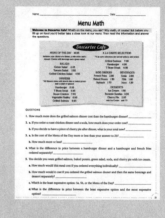

- pencil and paper
- calculator (optional)

### ANSWERS

**1.** 4.10
**2a.** 9.95
**2b.** 12.90
**3a.** less
**3b.** 1.95
**4.** 0.15
**5a.** 17.05
**5b.** 15.65
**5c.** Menu of the Day
**5d.** 6.10

## EXTENSION ACTIVITIES

This is an activity that segues nicely into discussions about tax and percents. Students can re-compute all of their answers based on the food and beverage tax in your state, for example. This can also lead to a discussion about tipping. Students can then compute tax and tip, and discuss the difference between the price on the menu and what they actually end up paying for the meal. Try giving your students a limit on the money they can spend. They can list the items they want to order, along with the prices. Remind them that they will also need to pay for tax and a tip! A variety of take-out menus could come in handy and provide endless "menu math" activities.

# Menu Math

**Welcome to Descartes Cafe!** What's on the menu, you ask? Why math, of course! But before you fill up on food you'd better take a close look at our menu. Then read the information and answer the questions.

## Descartes Cafe

### MENU OF THE DAY   10.95
Includes your choice of a dinner, a side order, and a dessert. Comes with beverage and a green salad.

#### SALADS
Green Salad   2.85
Tomato Salad   3.95
Grilled Chicken Salad   4.95

#### DINNERS
*All dinners come with french fries or baked potato and a salad or spinach

Hamburger   5.85
T-Bone Steak   8.95
Roast Chicken   7.95
Vegetable Medley   6.95
Grilled Salmon   9.95

### A LA CARTE SELECTION
*A la carte selections are served without side orders

Grilled Salmon   7.00
Hamburger   4.00
T-Bone Steak   6.50

#### SIDE ORDERS
French Fries   2.00
Baked Potato   1.50
Spinach   1.75

#### BEVERAGES
Soda   2.00
Milk   1.00
Juice   1.50

#### DESSERTS
Ice Cream   1.00
Brownie Sundae   3.95
Cherry Pie   2.95
with Ice Cream   add .75

## QUESTIONS

**1.** How much more does the grilled salmon dinner cost than the hamburger dinner? _____

**2. a.** If you order a roast chicken dinner and a soda, how much does your order cost? _____

   **b.** If you decide to have a piece of cherry pie after dinner, what is your total now? _____

**3. a.** Is the cost of the Menu of the Day more or less than your answer to 2b? _____

   **b.** How much more or less? _____

**4.** What is the difference in price between a hamburger dinner and a hamburger and french fries ordered separately? _____

**5.** You decide you want grilled salmon, baked potato, green salad, soda, and cherry pie with ice cream.

   **a.** How much would this meal cost if you ordered everything individually? _____

   **b.** How much would it cost if you ordered the grilled salmon dinner and then the same beverage and dessert separately? _____

   **c.** Which is the least expensive option: 5a, 5b, or the Menu of the Day? _____

   **d.** What is the difference in price between the least expensive option and the most expensive option? _____

# Have Stats, Will Travel

**\*NOTE:** This activity has four parts. This teacher page accompanies the next four reproducibles.

## Learning Objective

Students read for detail a variety of charts relating to travel

## DIRECTIONS

1. Distribute the four Have Stats, Will Travel reproducibles to students. The charts and tables reflect some of the information travelers might use as they're planning a trip abroad: plane fares, currency exchange rates, weather, and individual city statistics. However, you do not have to use all four together or in sequence. Each activity can easily stand on its own.

2. Explain to students that they will be seeing a variety of information relating to travel, and they will have to read carefully to find the information they need.

3. Review phrases such as "average," "at least," and "no more than" with students, and talk about what they mean.

4. Instruct students to look at the information being presented before they answer any questions. Once they feel comfortable with the chart or table, remind them to read each question carefully. The answers are much easier to find if the students are clear on what they are looking for.

## ANSWERS

**Page 53**
1. $278   **2a.** Westward Ho   **2b.** $582
3. Unrestricted fare from New York to Denver
**4a.** $2,942   **4b.** Far-and-Away   **4c.** $2,043   **5.** 9

**Page 54**
1. 7   **2a.** 49 degrees   **2b.** 19 degrees   **3.** average low in Delhi
**4a.** Cairo   **4b.** Mexico City   **5.** Hong Kong
**6a.** Edinburgh   **6b.** Delhi

**Page 55**
1. Canada; Australia; Hong Kong   **2.** Belgium; France
**3a.** 1,775.10   **3b.** 288.20   **4a.** shilling   **4b.** 56.09
**5.** Spanish pesetas   **6.** 79.18

**Page 56**
1. 89 degrees   **2.** 3.9 million   **3.** yes   **4a.** $1.41   **4b.** $3.41
**5a.** $10.30   **5b.** 35.6 kilometers

## ▲▲▲▲▲▲▲

## What You'll Need

- Have Stats, Will Travel reproducibles, pages 53–56

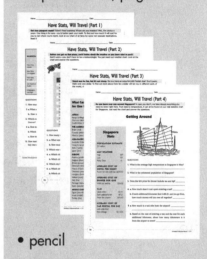

- pencil
- paper
- calculator

## ▼▼▼▼▼▼▼

## EXTENSION ACTIVITIES

The international flavor of these activities naturally lends itself to a great deal of multicultural exchange and learning. They also present a wonderful way to work on money math. Students could be given a travel budget and plan a trip—buy tickets, pay for transportation from the airport, and figure out how far their dollars will go in a certain country. Exchange rates are a great way to teach conversions, decimals, and calculator skills.

# Have Stats, Will Travel (Part 1)

**Got your passport ready?** Ticket? Final boarding! Where are you headed? Well, the choice is yours. One thing is for sure—you'd better pack your math. To find out how much it will cost for you to get where you're going, look at our chart of air fares for some very popular destinations. Read the information and answer the questions.

## Stats Take Flight!

### AIR FARES

| DOMESTIC ROUTES | Discount Fare; Airline | Unrestricted Fare; Airline | INTERNATIONAL ROUTES | Discount Fare; Airline | Unrestricted Fare; Airline |
|---|---|---|---|---|---|
| New York-Denver | $278: Fly Now | $1,828: Fly Now | New York-Athens | $730: Sky High | $1,682: Sky High |
| New York-Los Angeles | $318: Born2Fly | $682: Born2Fly | New York-Hong Kong | $1,210: Pacific Trails | $3,096: Pacific Trails |
| New York-St. Louis | $278: SkyWorld | $1,164: SkyWorld | Atlanta-Cape Town | $899: Far-and-Away | $2,942: Far-and-Away |
| San Francisco-Austin | $198: Westward Ho | $582: Westward Ho | Los Angeles-Moscow | $610: East Way | $1,150: East Way |
| Washington-Las Vegas | $198: Air Up There | $630: Air Up There | San Francisco-Mexico City | $379: Border Air | $480: Border Air |

## QUESTIONS

**1.** How much is a discount air fare from New York to St. Louis? _____

**2 a.** What airline is offering a flight from San Francisco to Austin? _____

**b.** How much is the unrestricted fare? _____

**3.** Which costs more, a discount flight from New York to Athens or an unrestricted fare from New York to Denver? _____

**4 a.** How much is an unrestricted fare from Atlanta to Cape Town? _____

**b.** Which airline provides that service? _____

**c.** How much more is the unrestricted fare than the discount fare? _____

**5.** How many discount tickets from New York to Los Angeles can be bought with the money required to buy one unrestricted ticket from New York to Hong Kong? _____

# Have Stats, Will Travel (Part 2)

**Before you get on that plane, you'd better check the weather so you know what to pack!**

Don't worry—you don't have to be a meteorologist. You just need our weather chart. Look at the chart and answer the questions.

## How's the Weather?

### May Days

| City | Average High/Low | Rainy Days | City | Average High/Low | Rainy Days |
|------|------------------|------------|------|------------------|------------|
| Athens | 77/61 | 8 | Los Angeles | 72/53 | 2 |
| Atlanta | 79/60 | 10 | Madrid | 70/50 | 10 |
| Beijing | 81/55 | 6 | Mexico City | 78/54 | 17 |
| Boston | 66/49 | 11 | Moscow | 66/46 | 13 |
| Buenos Aires | 64/47 | 7 | New York | 68/53 | 11 |
| Cairo | 91/63 | 0 | Paris | 68/49 | 12 |
| Chicago | 65/50 | 12 | Phoenix | 91/60 | 1 |
| Delhi | 105/79 | 2 | Rome | 74/56 | 5 |
| Dublin | 60/43 | 10 | San Juan | 84/74 | 16 |
| Edinburgh | 56/43 | 14 | Sydney | 66/52 | 13 |
| Hong Kong | 82/74 | 13 | Tokyo | 71/54 | 10 |
| Houston | 84/66 | 7 | Toronto | 63/44 | 13 |
| Jerusalem | 81/57 | 1 | Washington | 75/54 | 12 |
| London | 62/47 | 12 | Zurich | 67/47 | 14 |

QUESTIONS

**1.** How many rainy days were there in May in Buenos Aires? _____

**2. a.** What was the average low temperature in Paris? _____

   **b.** How much lower was Paris's average low temperature than the average high? _____

**3.** Which was warmer, the average low in Delhi or the average high in Sydney? _____

**4. a.** Which city had the least number of rainy days? _____

   **b.** Which city had the greatest? _____

**5.** Which city had the least temperature change between the high and low? _____

**6. a.** Which city had the lowest average high? _____

   **b.** Which city had the highest average low? _____

*Scholastic Professional Books • 2001*

# Have Stats, Will Travel (Part 3)

**Travel may be fun, but it's not cheap.** Do you have an extra 564,602 Turkish liras? Don't panic, that's only one dollar. To find out more about how far a dollar will get you in different parts of the world, check our currency exchange chart and answer the questions.

## Money and Math in Many Lands

### What Can You Get for One Dollar In? . . .

| | May 2000 | May 1999 |
|---|---|---|
| **AFRICA** | | |
| Kenya (shilling) | 56.09 | 50.90 |
| Morocco (dirham) | 9.02 | 8.34 |
| South Africa (rand) | 5.21 | 4.67 |
| **THE AMERICAS** | | |
| Brazil (real) | 1.64 | 1.51 |
| Canada (dollar) | 1.44 | 1.42 |
| Mexico (peso) | 8.85 | 8.75 |
| **ASIA-PACIFIC** | | |
| Australia (dollar) | 1.67 | 1.47 |
| Hong Kong (dollar) | 7.56 | 7.52 |
| India (rupee) | 40.42 | 39.59 |
| Japan (yen) | 104.78 | 116.30 |
| **EUROPE** | | |
| Austria (schilling) | 14.67 | 12.62 |
| Belgium (franc) | 43.01 | 36.98 |
| Britain (pound) | .63 | .60 |
| Denmark (krone) | 7.95 | 6.81 |
| France (franc) | 6.99 | 6.01 |
| Germany (mark) | 2.09 | 1.79 |
| Hungary (fornint) | 262.50 | 218.60 |
| Ireland (punt) | .80 | .69 |
| Italy (lira) | 2,063.30 | 1,775.10 |
| Portugal (escudo) | 203.70 | 175.30 |
| Spain (peseta) | 169.20 | 145.50 |
| **MIDDLE EAST** | | |
| Egypt (pound) | 3.18 | 3.15 |
| Israel (shekel) | 3.76 | 3.83 |
| Turkey (lira) | 564,602.00 | 32,972.00 |

### QUESTIONS

**1.** What countries besides the United States use a unit of currency called the dollar?

_____

_____

**2.** Which countries use a unit of currency called the franc? _____

_____

**3. a.** How many Italian liras could you get for one dollar in 1999? _____

**b.** How many more Italian liras could you get for one dollar in 2000? _____

**4. a.** What is the unit of currency in Kenya?

_____

**b.** How much of that currency could you get for a dollar in 2000? _____

**5.** If you had one dollar in 2000, which could you get more of, Japanese yen or Spanish pesetas? _____

**6.** In 1999, how many Indian rupees could you get with two dollars? _____

# Have Stats, Will Travel (Part 4)

**Do you know your way around Singapore?** In case you don't, we have almost everything you need to know right here. From taxis to temperature, it can all be found on our vital statistics chart for Singapore. Just read the chart and answer the questions.

## Getting Around

### Singapore Stats

**POPULATION ESTIMATE**
3.9 million

**MAY WEATHER**

| | |
|---|---|
| High | 89° |
| Low | 75° |
| Rainy Days | 15 |

**AVERAGE COST OF HOTEL PER NIGHT**
Room for one with tax $230.50

**AVERAGE COST OF DINNER FOR ONE**
With tax and tip       $24.00

**TAXI**

| | |
|---|---|
| Upon entry | $1.41 |
| Each additional km | $0.25 |
| From the airport | $10.30 |

**AVERAGE COST OF CAR RENTAL PER DAY**
with unlimited
free mileage       $113.56

### QUESTIONS

1. What is the average high temperature in Singapore in May?

   _____

2. What is the estimated population of Singapore?

   _____

3. Does the $24 price for dinner include tax and tip? _____

   _____

4. **a.** How much does it cost upon entering a taxi? _____

   **b.** If each additional kilometer (km) is $0.25, and you go 8 km, how much money will you owe all together? _____

   _____

5 **a.** How much is a taxi ride from the airport? _____

   _____

   **b.** Based on the cost of entering a taxi and the cost for each additional kilometer, about how many kilometers is it from the airport to town? _____

Scholastic Professional Books • 2001

# Statistics Scavenger Hunt

## Learning Objectives
Various

## DIRECTIONS

1. In this activity, students will be venturing around their class, school, or community looking for any evidence of statistics they can find. The objective is for students to become increasingly aware of the incredible amount of math surrounding them every day, whether or not they are in school.

2. Brainstorm with students all the various graphs, charts, and tables they can think of, and have them talk about where they've seen them. It's okay for them to mention some of the things that have been brought to their attention in this activity book, but encourage them to look around them for many sources of statistics: hospital charts; feature check-lists on the boxes of toys, games, and electronics; cook-books; automobile tune-up checklists; and so forth.

3. Tell students that they are going on a scavenger hunt to find examples of at least five different graphs, charts, or tables. Explain to students that they will earn points for each example they bring in, and that each example must be accompanied by one math question relating to the chart, table, or graph they've presented. The student who earns the most points in the allotted amount of time wins.

   **NOTE:** No points for bringing in two different versions of the same stat (for example: box scores from two different baseball games). It is very important that students under-stand what their graphs, charts, and tables represent. This is why the accompanying math question is a key part of this activity.

4. Keep a list of places where students have found statistical examples and post them in the classroom. This activity can go on for as long as you like. Once completed, results can be taped on the walls of the classroom and students can go around and complete the math questions that go along with each graph.

## What You'll Need

- pencil

- paper

## EXTENSION ACTIVITIES

This activity can be a team competition with groups of students competing to find the greatest number of charts, tables, or graphs possible within a strict time frame. Extra credit can be given if students create two different styles of graph using the same information, for example, taking part of the information given in a pie graph and turning it into a bar graph. To encourage creativity, prizes could be given for the most sur-prising stat or the best artistic represen-tation of a chart, table, or graph. Students should feel free to really go all-out, even creating a 3-D pictograph or doing an accompanying report on their topic for extra credit. Depending on the information presented in the various graphs, a great deal of learning beyond math can be shared. Have students pres-ent their favorite statistic—a mapping exercise of archaeological finds in Egypt, for example—and talk about what they learned about the topic behind the graph, chart, or table.

# Appendix 1: Quick Reference

## LINE GRAPH

**A line graph shows changes over time.**

Example: How sports participation in school has changed from 1970 to 2000.

## DOUBLE (OR MULTIPLE) LINE GRAPH

**A multiple line graph shows changes over time for two (or more) different groups.**

Example: How sports participation in school has changed from 1970 to 2000, with one line representing boys, the other, girls.

## BAR GRAPH

**A bar graph uses bars to show and compare total numbers of things.**

Example: The total number of Olympic gold medals won, with one bar representing the medal total of each country.

## DOUBLE BAR GRAPH

**A double bar graph uses bars to show total numbers of things, but divides each total number into two groups.**

Example: The total number of Olympic gold medals won by country, with each country represented by two bars, one bar for men's events, the other bar for women's.

## STACKED BAR GRAPH

**A stacked bar graph divides one piece of information, represented by one bar, into two specific parts.**

Example: One bar representing the total amount of money earned by an athlete, divided into money received from salary and money received from endorsements.

## CIRCLE GRAPH (OR PIE CHART)

**A circle graph shows parts of a whole.**

Example: The total circle represents the number of Super Bowl victories, divided into victories for AFC teams and victories for NFC teams.

## PICTOGRAPH

**A pictograph uses pictures. Each picture represents a certain number of people or things.**

Example: The total rainfall in inches for several different cities, with one umbrella equivalent to 2 inches of rainfall.

# Appendix 2: Teacher Resources

Here are places where you can find additional statistical information to use along with the blank graphing reproducibles (pages 61–64). Used together, you can create and interpret charts, tables, and graphs of your own. Some of these resources already present the information in graph form. The information either can be interpreted in the given form, or students can be challenged to present the information using another type of chart, table, or graph.

## SCHOLASTIC KIDS USA SURVEY

**www.scholastic.com/**

This site contains a poll of classrooms across the United States about issues concerning kids, including topics such as violence in the media, the environment, and school uniforms.

For more research information and other helpful teaching hints, take a look at what else is on www.scholastic.com. To get to Kids USA Survey from the home page, you can start by clicking on "Teachers," then "Online Activities," and finally "Math" and go from there.

## USA TODAY

**www.usatoday.com/snapshot/life/snapldex.htm**

In addition to the newspaper itself, *USA Today*'s Web site has an archive of its "Snapshots," the popular polls and graphs featured in the paper. Listed according to topic, the polls contain statistical information about everything from teen smoking to how many people prefer chunky to creamy peanut butter.

## U.S. CENSUS BUREAU

**www.census.gov**

More data than you'll know what to do with. Statistics on virtually every aspect of American life—poverty, education, population, ethnic breakdowns, and so forth.

## ALSO CHECK OUT THE SITE'S "POP CLOCK"

**www.census.gov/ftp/pub/main/www/popclock.html**

The "Pop Clock" has population updates from around the world every five minutes, and population estimates from 1950 to 2050.

## INFOPLEASE.COM

**www.infoplease.com**

A great place to start for any statistics activity—you could end up anywhere! The site has links to an exceptionally wide variety of almanacs, with information about geography, the entertainment world, politics, history, atlases and maps, and a K–12 Learning Network.

## CNN-SPORTS ILLUSTRATED

**www.cnnsi.com**

Sports is an ongoing source of statistical information and an area that usually appeals to kids. This is just one Web site that has statistical information for many sports. It includes team standings, schedules, points, and individual player statistics.

## BILLBOARD MAGAZINE

**www.billboard-online.com/charts**

*Billboard Magazine*'s Web site not only has the latest chart listing for hit music, but if you click on "This Week's Poll," you go to their "Voting Booth," where there are results of polls on current music topics.

## AMERICAN STOCK EXCHANGE

**www.amex.com**

Stocks are a great way to work with line graphs. The information also can be used to teach fractions and percents, as well as give kids some insight into economics.

## THE ENDANGERED SPECIES PROGRAM

**endangered.fws.gov**

Maps, charts, and statistical information about endangered animals and plants from the U.S. Fish and Wildlife Service's Division of Endangered Species.

## CENTER FOR DISEASE CONTROL'S TOBACCO INFORMATION AND PREVENTION SOURCEPAGE

**www.cdc.gov/nccdphp/osh/tobacco.htm**

A variety of statistics on a very important topic for kids. The site also contains information on smoking trends, current events, legislation, and how to stop smoking.

## NATIONAL CLIMATIC DATA CENTER

**www.ncdc.noaa.gov**

Weather information, with maps, charts, graphs, and tracking of weather systems. The site also features an interactive option that presents certain statistical information in graph form, if desired.

## OANDA.COM

**www.oanda.com**

Currency exchange and converter Web site. Charts featuring currency from all over the world. Many math tie-ins, including decimals. Also an excellent opportunity for cross-curricular tie-ins with geography, foreign languages, and social studies.

# Blank Graph Reproducibles

## PIE CHART
in 100 equal divisions

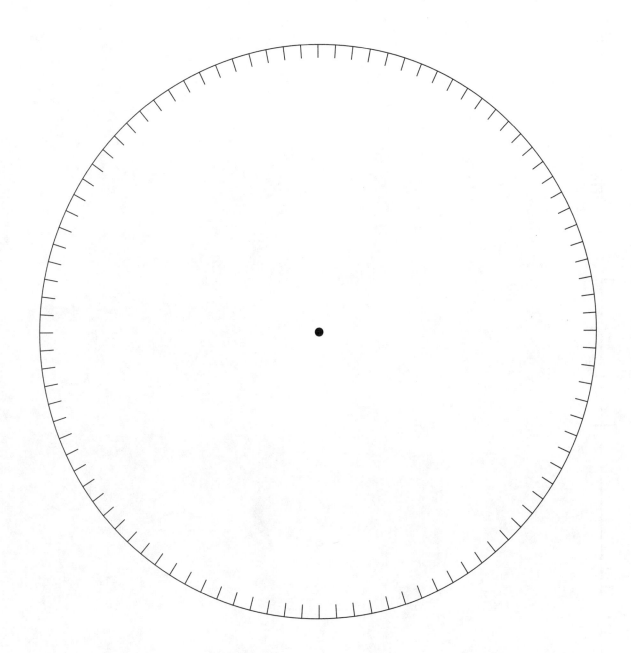

**AXIS 1**

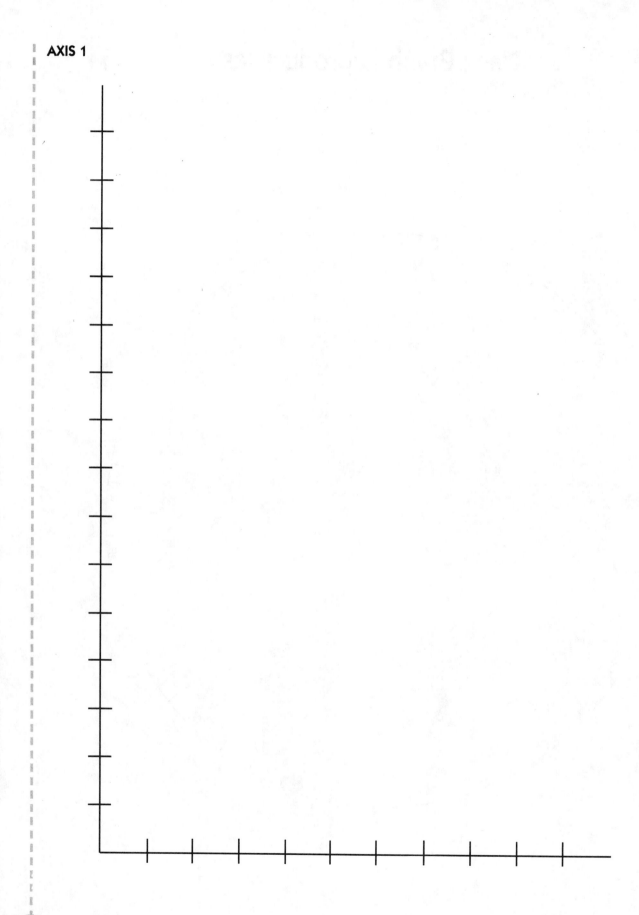

**AXIS 2**

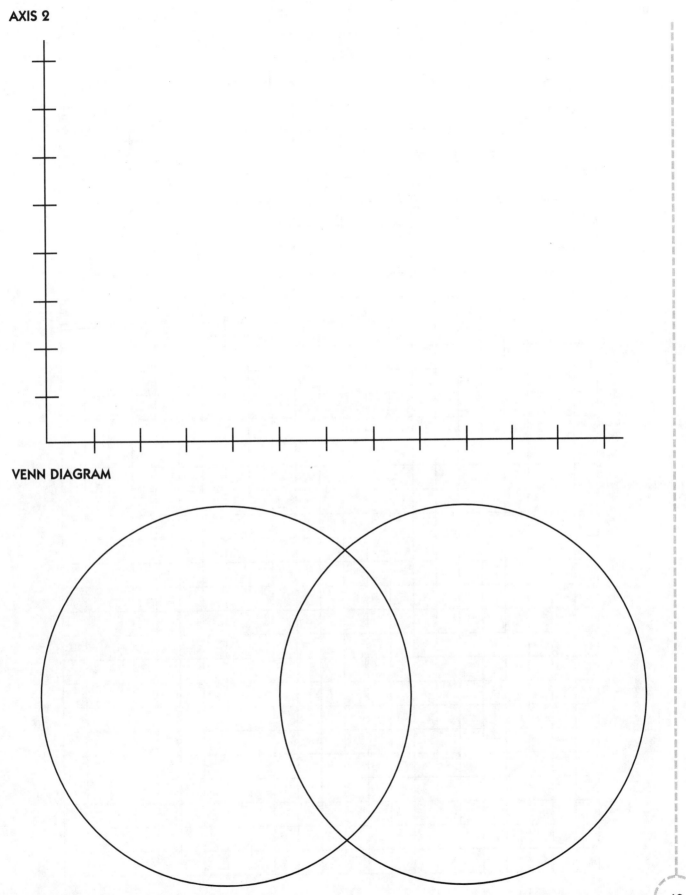

**VENN DIAGRAM**

**GRID**

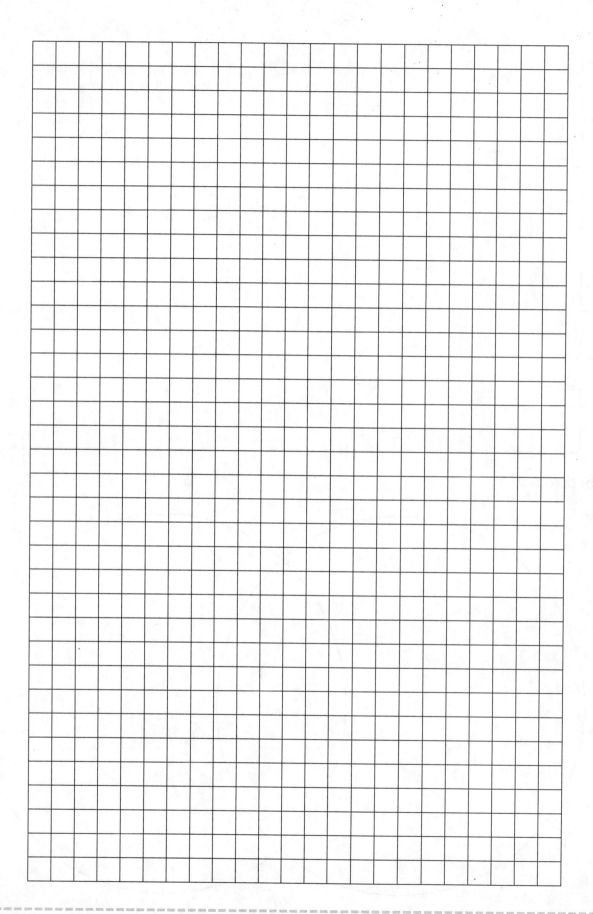

Scholastic Professional Books • 2001